JOBS IN THE
U.S. AIR FORCE

Published in 2023 by The Rosen Publishing Group, Inc.
29 East 21st Street, New York, NY 10010

First Edition

Portions of this work were originally authored by Earle Rice Jr. and Wilson Camelo and published as *Careers in the U.S. Air Force*. All new material in this edition was authored by Kyle Purrman.

Cataloging-in-Publication Data

Names: Purrman, Kyle.
Title: Jobs in the U.S. Air Force / Kyle Purrman.
Description: New York : Rosen Publishing, 2023. | Series: Exploring military careers | Includes glossary and index.
Identifiers: ISBN 9781499469899 (pbk.) | ISBN 9781499469905 (library bound) | ISBN 9781499469912 (ebook)
Subjects: LCSH: United States. Air Force--Juvenile literature. | United States. Air Force--Vocational guidance--Juvenile literature.
Classification: LCC UG633.P877 2023 | DDC 358.400973--dc23

Some of the images in this book illustrate individuals who are models. The depictions do not imply actual situations or events.

Manufactured in the United States of America

CPSIA Compliance Information: Batch #CSRYA23. For further information, contact Rosen Publishing, New York, New York, at 1-800-237-9932.

Find us on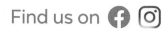

CONTENTS

CHAPTER 1

TAKING TO THE SKIES

Human air power is one of the greatest achievements in the modern world. The U.S. Air Force has helped the nation become a world leader because of its strength and mobility. In the 21st century, military careers in the United States are many and varied, with occupations available to anyone, whether they are interested in piloting a plane or working on computers. Cutting-edge technology helps keep the U.S. Air Force up and running.

Today's impressive fighters and bombers could never have existed if not for the work of Wilbur and Orville Wright, the American innovators who first took humanity to the skies in a plane. The Wright brothers' research and development took place mainly between 1899 and 1903 near Kitty Hawk, North Carolina. Orville's first successful flight lasted just 12 seconds, and Wilbur followed up with a liftoff that lasted nearly a minute. These seemingly small steps marked humanity's first real progress toward the age of flight.

FLYING PIONEERS

The Wright brothers were not the first to fly a craft that was heavier than air. For more than a century, people had been flying with balloons and gliders. For many years, the primary issue was not how to get a vessel airborne; the problems were more related to steering the craft and landing it safely when the pilot was ready.

In 1908, the U.S. Army purchased an advanced steerable airship—called a dirigible—that could stay in the air for two hours and fly at a speed of 20 miles (32.2 km) per hour. Later that same year, Orville Wright demonstrated the flight of a plane for army authorities. Unfortunately, the plane crashed and killed Lieutenant Thomas Selfridge, a signal corpsman. He was the first casualty in U.S. military aviation.

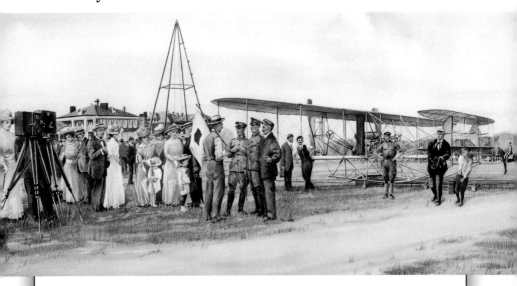

Brothers Wilbur and Orville Wright were the pioneering inventors who contributed to the development of the air force.

Airplane technology was not receiving great reviews in the United States, especially after the deadly 1908 demonstration, and U.S. leaders did not see how planes could help the military. The Wright brothers instead looked toward Europe to promote their accomplishment. British, French, German, and Italian military forces were quick to accept these new aircraft into their arsenals.

The U.S. Army finally purchased its first airplane from the Wright brothers in 1909. The brothers themselves trained the first military pilots. Early results showed that soldiers could effectively shoot and bomb targets from the air, but the army still did not think aircraft would be used for anything more than reconnaissance. In 1912, the army announced that it would stop funding aviation experiments.

As a result, the United States did not use aircraft in combat until 1916, when General John Pershing led an unsuccessful mission to find and capture Mexican revolutionary Pancho Villa. Across the ocean, World War I was raging across much of Europe, and aviation would play an important role in that conflict.

WORLD WAR I FROM ABOVE

World War I—called the "war to end all wars"—had been ongoing for almost three years when the United States entered the fray in 1917. Though the U.S. military was strong, its aviation unit had only 131 officers, of whom just 26 were considered fully trained. The nation had no combat aircraft, no units trained in warfare, and no pilots with actual combat experience. European pilots, in contrast, had been gaining experience for three years.

When it entered the war, the United States had no plans to build a full-scale air service that could fight in Europe, and it was not developing the capability to quickly build fighter aircraft. In the year before the United States entered the war, civilian factories had delivered only 64 of the 366 planes ordered. About a month after the United States entered the war, President Woodrow Wilson received a request from French premier Alexandre Ribot that America send 4,500 planes and 5,000 pilots to the front by spring 1918. This request kick-started the army's aviation expansion.

THE LOST BATTALION

In Europe, American pilots underwent training with their Allied counterparts and flew numerous reconnaissance missions in the fall of 1918. On a morning in early October 1918, the 50th Aero Squadron was deployed to find and bring supplies to three battalions of the 77th Division. Flying low in fog and amid hostile fire, the 50th went searching for a missing battalion. They successfully dropped supplies where they thought the Allied battalion was, but the supplies were instead claimed by Germans.

The next morning, Lieutenants Harold Goettler and Erwin Bleckley took off in their DH-4 aircraft to continue searching. They flew back to where they thought the battalion was located, but they were attacked as they arrived. The lieutenants retreated to the airfield for repairs and again returned to the area, but German gunners were waiting. Goettler and Bleckley were shot down and killed, both later receiving the Medal of Honor for their bravery. The day after the pilots were killed, survivors of the "Lost Battalion" were located.

Among the most famous World War I–era aviation commanders is General William "Billy" Mitchell. Concerned that units were being sent into combat without enough real experience, Mitchell took charge of training the First Army Air Service. Before long, he was in control of the largest group of air forces ever assembled in a single operation. Mitchell's 1,481 aircraft and 30,000 men were drawn from American, French, Italian, and British forces.

General Billy Mitchell was one of the first American commanders to understand that airpower could turn the tide of battle.

The first battle for the First Army Air Service was waged from September 12 to September 16, 1918. The results were impressive. American pilots conducted more than 3,000 flights over enemy lines, fired 30,000 rounds, made more than 1,000 bomb attacks, and destroyed 12 enemy balloons and 60 planes. The battle also produced the first two American "aces": Captain Eddie Rickenbacker and Second Lieutenant Frank Luke.

The final American air victory of World War I occurred on November 10, 1918, when Major Maxwell Kirby shot down a German Fokker craft while flying his Spad 13 plane during a patrol mission. Kirby attacked the unsuspecting enemy pilot from above. World War I came to an end the next day.

Though the United States joined the war quite late, American aviators were credited with destroying 776 enemy planes and 72 enemy balloons. Pilots took more than 18,000 photographs and dropped 275,000 pounds (125,000 km) of bombs. In comparison, 290 U.S. planes and 37 balloons were lost. The United States also had 569 battle casualties, 164 aviators killed in action, 102 captured, and 200 missing in action.

BETWEEN THE WARS

The U.S. military learned many lessons about airpower during World War I. As technology continued to advance, military commanders began to develop ways to fight future wars, which would likely use more aerial strategies. General Mitchell returned from Europe after the war, ready to play a role in shaping the future of airpower. He discovered, however, that his position as director of military aeronautics had been removed by General Charles Menoher, chief of the air service. In addition, Congress slashed the air service from 200,000 people to only 10,000. General Menoher told manufacturers that the United States was done spending money on new aircraft. Originally projected to be $83 million, the budget for aviation was cut to just $25 million. Meanwhile, Britain increased its spending to $350 million.

Mitchell criticized these actions. He believed that the country needed to develop a separate air force. He claimed to Congress that he could destroy any navy ship, and that for the cost of one battleship they could buy 1,000 bombers. In response, Congress had the navy provide Mitchell with old ships he could use for testing. The navy thought Mitchell would fail.

In February 1921, Mitchell gathered hundreds of men and 250 airplanes at Langley Field in Virginia to practice. The testing day was June 21, using the German battleship *Ostfriesland* as the target ship. The navy considered the ship "unsinkable." In just over 20 minutes, however, the planes successfully bombed and sank the *Ostfriesland*, earning Mitchell instant fame around the world.

Soon after, Mitchell went to the Pacific to gather information. He found that intelligence services were not cooperating well. Based on his own observations—regarding Japan's industrial growth and increasing air power—he concluded that the Japanese could soon be an aerial threat to the United States. When he returned to the United States in 1924, he was disappointed that the air service was still in poor shape and that his predictions about Japan were not taken seriously. Mitchell loudly continued to voice his disagreements with the government's actions until President Calvin Coolidge ordered him court-martialed.

His trial lasted seven weeks, but the jury took less than an hour to find Mitchell guilty on all charges. He was sentenced to a reduced rank and loss of pay for five years. He retired instead. Mitchell was later vindicated when many of his predictions about air-power came true.

THE RISE OF NUCLEAR POWER

By the time Japanese planes were dropping the first bombs on Pearl Harbor on December 7, 1941, air power's role in the military was well established. At the time of the Pearl Harbor attack, there were more than 200 army air force planes in Hawaii. Some were classified as fighter aircraft. Others, like the B-17, were bombers. Regardless of class, less than half of the aircraft in Hawaii were considered fully operational.

The Pearl Harbor attack forced the United States—which had remained separate from the quickly spreading World War II—into the conflict. The navy and air force saw most of their action in the

The Japanese attack on Pearl Harbor not only pushed the United States into World War II but also proved the importance of a strong air fleet.

Pacific, fighting Japanese control over the seas and skies. It was important to control islands throughout the South Pacific because U.S. aircraft did not have enough range to reach Japan from Hawaii. They would need islands in between at which they could stop to refuel.

In April 1942, the United States got revenge by carrying out an innovative air strike on mainland Japan. Lieutenant Colonel Jimmy Doolittle came up with a plan to launch B-25 bombers from the deck of the navy carrier *Hornet*. The soldiers who volunteered were told only that this would be the most dangerous mission of their lives. Crews trained at Eglin Field in Florida by taking off from a patch of airstrip marked with the width and length of the *Hornet*'s deck.

Doolittle's plan was to launch the B-25s about 400 miles (644 km) from the Japanese coast, have them bomb targets in Japan, and then land in either China or Russia. Landing in Japan was not an option. To make the planes as light as possible to preserve fuel, most of the B-25s' guns and equipment were removed.

After months of careful planning, on the day of the attack, April 18, 1942, the *Hornet* was spotted by a Japanese boat. Instead of the planned 400 miles, the planes would have to fly from 650 miles (1,046 km) away. Doolittle personally led the attack as the first B-25 pilot to take off from the *Hornet*. The bombers struck Tokyo and other Japanese cities. Many B-25 crews, low on fuel, bailed out, leading to one crewman's death. Only one B-25 landed safely in the Soviet Union. Three planes had to come down in Japanese-occupied China; the crews were later executed. Though the overall damage to Japan was not severe, the attack gave the enemy a scare and provided the American people a much-needed morale boost. Doolittle was promoted to brigadier general and later awarded the Medal of Honor.

In Europe, army air force aircraft and personnel were sent to support the Allies against Germany. Here again, bombers would play a significant role, turning the tide of the war.

The one way to defeat Germany was to destroy its military-industrial capabilities. At the time, bombing was highly inaccurate, the weather in Europe was poor, and bombers had to fly to their targets at very high altitudes to avoid anti-aircraft artillery. With all these obstacles, it often took hundreds of bombers to fly a single mission to destroy a target. In addition, fighter planes, used as escorts, could not carry enough fuel to escort the bombers all the way to the target. Many bombers were shot down, and morale was low among bomber pilots. However, bombers and fighters had an undeniable effect in the war.

On June 6, 1944, the United States launched the D-Day invasion against German forces in Europe. Allied air forces conducted bombing missions ahead of American ground troops that were staging attacks in places like Normandy, France. Fighters provided aerial support for infantry troops, cargo aircraft carried critical equipment and supplies, and other crafts dropped paratroopers behind enemy lines. This massive assault led to Germany's eventual surrender on May 8, 1945, also called VE day.

Even after VE day, however, fighting continued with Japan in the Pacific. It was not until B-29 bombers dropped atomic bombs on the Japanese cities of Hiroshima and Nagasaki that the fighting came to a close. World War II ended on August 15, 1945. During the course of U.S. involvement in the war, 40,000 army air force members were killed in action and another 15,000 were killed in training or accidents in the United States.

CHAPTER 2

EXPANDING THE AIR FORCE

Though the U.S. military increasingly used aircraft in battle during World War I and World War II, the nation was still hesitant to dedicate an entire branch of the armed services to airpower. Leaders like General Billy Mitchell and General Henry H. "Hap" Arnold advocated for an independent air force, but they were often ignored. It was not until the conclusion of the Second World War that President Harry Truman pushed for a military overhaul. In 1947, the National Security Act reorganized the nation's defense system, combining the Department of War and the Department of the Navy and establishing an independent air force. This new branch would soon face a tough challenge overseas, as the Soviet Union made moves against the United States and its allies. The Cold War between these global powers had begun.

JET POWER IN KOREA

In June 1950, North Korean troops and tanks charged south across the 38th parallel toward Seoul, the capital of the Republic of Korea. The United Nations (UN)—at the time a newly formed international organization—called on its members to fight for South Korea. It was going to take time for enough American troops to be deployed to South Korea, and in the meantime, the Far East Air Force was largely responsible for its defense.

The United States had entered the jet era, but other nations also had capable airplanes. The first effective combat jet was the Russian MiG-15. Soon, the air force introduced the F-80 Shooting Star and F-86 Sabre to face the Russian fighters in areas known as "MiG Alley," a Communist stronghold in northwest Korea.

Aircraft advanced quickly in the 20th century, and the Russian MiG-15 is regarded as the first truly effective combat jet.

At first, the air force mainly provided defensive support. On October 7, 1950, however, President Harry Truman authorized U.S. troops to pursue North Korean forces who were retreating across the 38th parallel. American and South Korean soldiers entered the North Korean capital of Pyongyang on October 19. Far East Air Force B-29s and B-26s bombed targets in North Korea, while B-26s, F-51s, and F-80s provided close air support for ground troops.

After years of negotiations, fighting in the Korean War stopped on July 27, 1953. More than 50,000 Americans had died in the war. The boundary line between North and South Korea remained at the 38th Parallel, where the two sides had fought to a stalemate.

LEARNING IN BATTLE

The United States entered the Cold War relatively unprepared in the air. In 1952, however, the air force invested in new fighter models, replacing many of its F-86Es with F-86Fs. The F-86F had more powerful engines and improved wing edges, helping them better compete with the MiG-15. As the conflict continued, the Communists limited their flights to MiG Alley and tried to avoid aerial combat with F-86 pilots. By August and September, however, MiG pilots had become frustrated and more aggressive, and aerial engagements occurred almost daily. U.S. pilots generally had the upper hand in these battles. From May to June 1953, F-86F fighters claimed 165 aerial victories while losing only 3 aircraft.

After the Korean War, the United States kicked off an arms and space race with the Soviet Union. The Soviets were the first nation to reach space when they launched their satellite *Sputnik* in 1957. The first man in space was also a Soviet cosmonaut. Not to be outdone, the United States followed by putting its own manned spacecraft into orbit. President John F. Kennedy pledged to have a man on the moon by 1969. Though Kennedy did not live to see an American reach the moon, President Richard Nixon followed through on that promise: NASA's historic landing took place in 1969.

In addition to competing in space exploration, Soviets and Americans were fighting over nuclear power. Hundreds of missiles were spread all throughout the world, and both sides were kept in check by a simple principle of "mutually assured destruction." Because both sides had enough nuclear weapons to

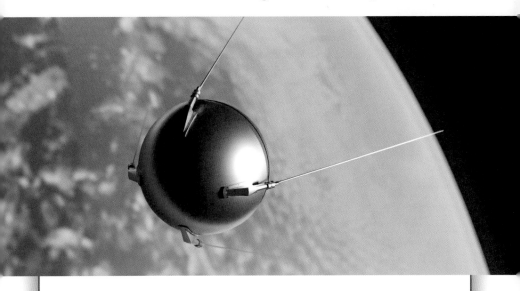

The Soviet Union got out to an early lead in the race to the stars, putting both a satellite and a man into space before the United States.

destroy the world, one attacking the other would mean the end of humanity.

The United States and the Soviet Union seemed to have reached a standstill until 1962, when air force U-2 spy planes flying over Cuba came back with images of Russian missile sites under construction. Cuba, located very close to the U.S. eastern seaboard, could have been the perfect staging ground for a Soviet assault. For the first time, nuclear war seemed like a real possibility. President Kennedy placed Cuba under a quarantine, establishing an aerial and naval blockade of supplies to the island. The world held its breath. Eventually, Russian premier Nikita Khrushchev backed down.

President Kennedy was quick to call on the increasingly powerful air force to deal with the Cuban Missile Crisis.

AN EASTERN RUMBLING

In 1954, Vietnam was split in half after revolution-aries defeated the French, who had colonized the country. In the north, a Communist regime gained power; in the south, an anti-Communist leader took charge. Soon after defeating France, the two sides resumed fighting. In 1961, worried about the spread of Communism throughout Asia, the United States began training the South Vietnamese armed forces to fight the northerners. The U.S. military also began conducting active operations, such as reconnaissance.

Toward the end of 1961, President Kennedy's advisers recommended that the U.S. become more involved in Vietnam. By 1963, there were 15,000 American soldiers in Vietnam. Under President Lyndon B. Johnson in 1964, the United States began a bombing campaign. Leaders in Washington, D.C., thought that bombings would be a sufficient show of force to intimidate the enemy and bring an end to the conflict.

However, North Vietnamese leaders never believed that Americans were committed enough to be a threat. Although the Vietnam War saw more bombs dropped than all of World War II, much of the destruction was ineffective. American political leaders did not want to target civilian areas, making it easy for North Vietnamese to take cover during bombing runs.

In 1965, the United States launched an air cam-paign called Rolling Thunder. This campaign planned to use aircraft like the F-105 and the F-4 Phantom to strike targets over cities. North Vietnamese forces countered with aircraft like MiG-17s and MiG-21s, but their anti-aircraft and surface-to-air missiles were a bigger threat, claiming many U.S. aircraft and crews. In 1966 alone, the air force lost more than 2,000 aircraft.

The Vietnam War stretched across Johnson's presidency and into Richard Nixon's. When Nixon took office in 1969, he continued discussions to end the war. However, he suspended peace talks at one point and authorized a major air campaign: Operation Linebacker. It was the most effective use of the air force in Vietnam because it destroyed many of the targets that were previously considered off-limits for political reasons. When peace talks resumed—and then failed again—the Americans launched Operation Linebacker II. Fifteen B-52 bombers were lost during the 11 day offensive, but it proved what the air force could achieve during the war if used aggressively. In January 1973, negotiations to end the war restarted, and an agreement was finally signed. American soldiers were headed home by March. Two years later, the Communists had unified all of Vietnam under their power.

FIGHTING IN THE DESERT

In August 1990, Saddam Hussein's Iraqi military invaded neighboring Kuwait, a nation rich with oil with easy access to the Persian Gulf. A small group of U.S. Air Force fighter jets were the only obstacle standing between Saddam's forces and the oil fields of nearby Saudi Arabia.

OPERATION DESERT SHIELD

Immediately after the invasion, the UN demanded that Saddam leave Kuwait. When Saddam refused, the United States and its allies launched Operation Desert Shield. This was a campaign to build up international military strength in the region. Soon, thousands of U.S. and foreign troops and aircraft were deployed to several countries in the Middle East. This show of force was meant to demonstrate to Saddam that the world was serious about forcing Iraq out of Kuwait. Desert Shield was also meant to prevent Iraq from invading other countries.

The air force contributed some of its newest weapons, including the F-117 stealth fighter. It was classified as a "stealth" aircraft because it was designed to deflect and absorb radar. In addition, a new line of "smart bombs" was introduced. These bombs used satellites, radar, and lasers to guide them to a target.

Iraqi dictator Saddam Hussein was at the heart of Middle Eastern conflicts in the 1990s and early 2000s.

President George H. W. Bush issued an order to Saddam: Remove Iraqi troops from Kuwait by January 17, 1991, or face a massive attack. Saddam ignored the order, and as the deadline passed, Operation Desert Shield became Operation Desert Storm. A wave of F-117 stealth fighters soon entered Iraqi airspace undetected and bombed targets in Baghdad, the nation's capital. Though the F-117 had been used before, the Persian Gulf War was the first time the world truly saw the capabilities of stealth technology.

Air force fighter and bomber aircraft began targeting Iraq's infrastructure, including power plants, bridges, and communication posts. Saddam's forces were essentially left defenseless. Unable to communicate with his generals and forced to flee from bunker to bunker every night, Saddam saw his military fall apart. Thousands of troops surrendered to international coalition forces, and what was left of Saddam's air force escaped to Iran. After weeks of aerial bombing, the ground offensive began. It lasted only 100 hours. Iraqi forces were driven out of Kuwait and Operation Desert Storm was over.

SERBIAN ACTION

After being elected in 1989, Yugoslav president Slobodan Milosevic imposed Serbian rule in a small Serbian province called Kosovo. Milosevic began violently oppressing the ethnic Kosovar Albanians, resulting in the death of more than 250,000 civilians by 1995.

In 1998, Milosevic ordered an attack against an Albanian resistance force called the Kosovo Liberation Army. Nearly 100 civilians were killed in the attack. After witnessing the violence, the United States sent an ambassador to Belgrade, Serbia, hoping to negotiate with Milosevic to stop targeting civilians. When Milosevic refused, the UN passed Security Council Resolution 1199, calling for the end to the conflict. Milosevic initially agreed to let a North Atlantic Treaty Organization (NATO) group into Kosovo to ensure that he followed the resolution, but he continued his violence against the Albanians. After more failed attempts to convince Milosevic to negotiate—and outraged by the violence committed in Kosovo—the United States and NATO gave Milosevic an ultimatum to stop his actions or face the consequences.

Milosevic refused to comply, and war began. However, this would not be an ordinary war. Neither NATO nor Congress wanted to engage in a ground war, which could result in many combat casualties, so President Bill Clinton called for the conflict to be fought solely from the air. On March 24, 1999, the first all-air mission, named Operation Allied Force, was launched.

The first phase of this operation was to take out the country's integrated air defense system and other targets to help NATO attack from the air with mini-mum collateral damage. The mountainous Serbian terrain was challenging for bombing, and the weather was often cloudy. This meant precision-guided munitions (PGMs) would be the weapons of choice. During Operation Desert Storm, only 10 percent of the aircraft were capable of launching PGMs. During Operation Allied Force, that number was closer to 90 percent.

Operation Allied Force saw the combat debut of the B-2 stealth bomber. It was also the first conflict in which the air force used its three heavy bombers—the B-2, B-52, and B-1—at the same time in combat. All told, these craft delivered 11,000 out of the more than 23,000 U.S. bombs during the conflict. B-2s flew nonstop from Whiteman Air Force Base in Missouri to Kosovo, conducting missions to drop satellite-guided bombs on enemy targets that lasted around 30 hours.

The B-2 stealth bomber is an iconic air force plane, and it first saw action during the conflict in Kosovo.

In June 1999, Operation Allied Force came to an end when Milosevic agreed to allow 50,000 troops from NATO countries into Serbia. In total, crews from allied nations flew nearly 40,000 sorties. Of these, more than 23,000 were combat missions. At the turn of the century, the air force was proving to the world how formidable it could be.

CHAPTER 3

A MODERN FLEET

After the Soviet Union broke apart in 1989 and 1991's Gulf War came to an end, President George H. W. Bush started to push for a smaller military. Now that a time period of intense conflict had ended, many believed it was time to reduce the military accordingly. President Bill Clinton followed this trend, cutting jobs and funding dramatically between 1992 and 2000. Though the U.S. military was not actively engaged in full-scale conflicts during this time, it still had ongoing duties. After being cut by nearly 30 percent, the air force and its members were stretched thin. As part of an effort toward making the fleet more modern, American leaders began thinking about how to make better use of its airpower resources.

NEW DIVISIONS

On August 4, 1998, Air Force Secretary F. Whitten Peters and Air Force Chief of Staff General Michael Ryan announced that there would be a new way of organizing the air force. As soon as it was ready, the air force would split its combat and support assets into 10 aerospace expeditionary forces (AEFs).

Each AEF would comprise the weapon systems, pilots, support staff, and commanders needed to complete missions anywhere in the world. Specific pairs of AEFs would be on call for 90 days every 15 months, ready to respond to world events. For example, AEFs 1 and 2 would be ready to deploy if needed from January to March; AEFs 3 and 4 would be on call from April to June, and so on. Air force soldiers and aircraft were assigned to one of the AEFs, so they knew exactly when they would be on call to deploy.

The AEF concept was finally implemented in January 2000. Though the AEF system helped air force members deal with deployments and small-scale crisis events, AEFs were not designed for fighting a major global event. If full-scale war or a major crisis broke out, there would be a shortage of resources. The September 11 attacks were one such crisis. After the attacks, the AEF system was temporarily abandoned to better deal with the conflict.

In July 2003, AEFs returned. However, in response to increased needs around the world, Air Force Chief of Staff General John Jumper extended

The air force was quick to put the AEF system on hold in the wake of the September 11 attacks so that it could better respond to threats in the Middle East.

AEF on call periods to 120 days, up from the original 90 days. This meant airmen and women would be away from home for an additional month. However, the original 15-month rotation cycle was stretched to 20 months, so there was more time between deployments.

The AEF concept has generally been a success, and one reason is that AEFs make good use of the resources available to the air force, including the Air

Force Reserve (AFR) and Air National Guard (ANG). Members of the AFR and ANG are not full-time soldiers. Instead, they log a certain number of part-time hours of training and duty each month, and stand ready to be deployed if called upon. Most maintain regular jobs at civilian businesses. In 2004, ANG and AFR soldiers made up almost 14 percent of the total air force population. There were 107,000 ANG and 75,800 AFR troops compared to 359,000 active-duty airmen and women. When factoring in aircraft, supplies, and equipment, the reserves make up nearly half of the air force's total resources.

Though reservists commit only part of their time to military service, they play a major role in keeping the nation safe.

WAITING IN RESERVE

In the early 2000s, ANG and AFR airmen and women were fighting side by side with their active-duty counterparts more than ever before—and for longer periods of time. This created a significant strain on reservists' civilian employers. Organizations such as the Employer Support for Guard and Reserve assist reservists and their civilian employers as they deal with the increased time away from the office. The Uniformed Services Employment and Reemployment Rights Act (USERRA) established job protection for National Guard and reserve members. It ensures that employers cannot punish reservists who are deployed. USERRA also protects employers by ensuring that they are notified of upcoming deployments.

Today, the AFR has bases in various locations around the world. The AFR currently performs about 20 percent of the work of the air force.

FLYING GLOBAL SKIES

The air force is the primary service that protects U.S. airspace through Operation Noble Eagle (ONE). A total of 10 ANG fighter wings are spread out in three air defense sectors around the nation. The air force ensures that the United States is protected from aerial attack by flying combat air patrols over major U.S. cities. It also provides air support during major events, such as presidential inaugurations and the Super Bowl. From September 11, 2001, to March 2003, ANG, AFR, and active-duty air force units participating in ONE flew more than 25,000 fighter, tanker, and airborne early-warning missions.

The air force also maintains an international combat presence. Since the end of the Korean War in the 1950s, U.S. airborne units have been deployed in South Korea. Known as the 7th Air Force, this fighting unit is based at Osan Air Base in South Korea. The force includes F-16s (based at Kunsan Air Base in South Korea), A-10s, F-16s, HH-60G helicopters, and U-2 reconnaissance aircraft. Some airmen and women stationed at Osan Air Base have the choice of doing a one-year tour by themselves, or a two-year tour with family if they are married or have children.

After fighting in Serbia ended in 1999, the air force under U.S. European Command has provided soldiers, aircraft, and general support to the NATO-led troops in Kosovo. This international peacekeeping force includes contributions from the United States, Britain, France, Germany, and other countries. Though the force's responsibilities have mainly been given back to Kosovan authorities, the air force was instrumental in bringing stability to the region.

The F-16 is one of the most recognizable air force crafts, and it has been deployed all over the globe.

CHAPTER 4

THE AIR FORCE POWER STRUCTURE

There are many ways of dividing up and looking at the U.S. Air Force's military structure. At a lower level, air force major commands comprise smaller numbered air forces, which are themselves made up of "wings." These wings can further be divided into smaller groups, each of which is responsible for handling some duty at an air force base. Squadrons are the next smallest, and "flights" are the units that make up squadrons.

At a higher level, the air force operates as a part of the Department of the Air Force, which in turn is part of the larger Department of Defense. The air force is led by a secretary (a civilian) and supervised by a chief of staff (a military member); they report to the secretary of defense, who is directly beneath the president of the United States.

MAJOR COMMANDS AROUND THE WORLD

Each of the air force's major commands—also called MAJCOMs—is responsible for a specific function of the air force. Examples of these areas of expertise include training troops, fixing airplanes, and deploying fighter and bomber forces.

Air Combat Command (ACC) is the largest MAJCOM. It is headquartered at Langley Air Force Base in Virginia. ACC is responsible for fighters, bombers, attack, reconnaissance, battle management, electronic-combat aircraft, and command-and-control systems. Noteworthy aircraft used by ACC include the B-2 stealth fighter, the F-117 stealth fighter, and the F-22.

ACC has access to the most impressive and powerful aircraft the air force has to offer, including the F-117.

Between military and civilian employees, there are around 100,000 members of ACC. In addition, ACC includes more than 50,000 Air National Guardsmen and women and more than 10,000 air force reservists.

ACC operates out of 12 bases, organized into four numbered air forces (the 1st Air Force, 8th Air Force, 9th Air Force, and 12th Air Force). ACC has three major subunits and supervises the Air and Space Expeditionary Force Center.

Air Education and Training Command (AETC) is headquartered at Randolph Air Force Base in Texas. As its name implies, AETC oversees recruiting, training, and education for all air force soldiers. This includes basic military training, technical training, flying training, and professional military and degree-track professional education.

AETC also conducts basic military training for enlisted members; the U.S. Air Force Academy, Reserve Officer Training Corps (ROTC), or Officer Training School (OTS) for officers; and flight training. Air University (AU) at Maxwell Air Force Base in Alabama also falls under AETC. AU is the main hub for air force officer training programs, such as ROTC, Junior ROTC, and OTS, and the Civil Air Patrol. There are more than 70,000 active-duty, ANG, AFR, civilians, and contract workers in AETC.

Air Force Global Strike Command (AFGSC) calls Barksdale Air Force Base in Louisiana its home. AFGSC is responsible for three intercontinental ballistic wings: two B-52 wings and the only B-2 wing. AFGSC provides combat-ready forces for nuclear deterrence and global strike operations.

The B-52, which has been around since the 1950s, is an iconic aircraft still used by the air force for bombing missions.

Air Force Materiel Command (AFMC) is based at Wright-Patterson Air Force Base and operates three major product centers to acquire, develop, test, and deploy air-delivered weapons. These weapons range from missiles to command-and-control systems used to fight wars. AFMC also manages programs for everything from new weapon systems to retiring weapon platforms.

AFMC supervises air logistics and test centers like the Aircraft Maintenance and Regeneration Center, the Air Force Research Laboratory, the Air Force Test Pilot School, and the Air Force School of Aerospace Medicine.

AFMC is also in charge of the Air Force Flight Test Center (AFFTC) at Edwards Air Force Base in California. A world-renowned air technology center, the AFFTC conducts aerospace research, development, tests, and evaluation in support of the United States and its allies. When Chuck Yeager broke the sound barrier in 1947, he did so at the AFFTC.

Reserve forces are an important part of the U.S. military. The headquarters for Air Force Reserve Command (AFRC) is at Dobbins Air Reserve Base in Georgia. Reservists, nicknamed "citizen airmen," perform very similar functions to active-duty airmen. The more than 100,000 members of the AFRC are split into three numbered air forces (4th Air Force, 10th Air Force, and 22nd Air Force).

Many reservists are air reserve technicians (ARTs). ARTs work as military civilians during the week. Some have the same job during reserve weekends as they have during the regular workweek.

Chuck Yeager, a decorated air force officer and pilot, became the first human to break the sound barrier at AFFTC.

AFRC is typically only called on to supply airmen and aircraft during a national emergency. However, reserve units also provide support in peacetime. In general, reserve forces are divided into two groups: the Ready Reserve and the Standby Reserve. The Ready Reserve is called to fight in any emergency, while the Standby Reserve is only called on in a time of war.

The smallest MAJCOM, with fewer than 20,000 soldiers, is Air Force Special Operations Command (AFSOC). This command provides special weapons and tactics for the air force. AFSOC missions include information warfare, rescue operations, and specialized refueling. AFSOC also carries out psychological operations, using information and intelligence against an enemy to destroy its will to fight. In Iraq, for example, AFSOC units airdropped booklets over enemy territory, informing soldiers and civilians that Saddam Hussein was the enemy— not the Iraqi people. These leaflets also instructed people on how to surrender. AFSOC operates out of three locations in the United States and Japan.

United States Air Forces Central Command (USAFCENT) is the air element of United States Central Command (USCENTCOM), a regional unified command. USAFCENT is generally responsible for air operations, whether pilots are working alone or with cooperation from soldiers from allied countries. It is also tasked with developing backup plans in support of national objectives for USCENTCOM's area of responsibility (AOR) in Southwest Asia, which includes 20 countries. Additionally, USAFCENT manages supply lines and equipment logistics programs at several AOR sites.

The massive aircraft that transport troops and carry equipment are part of the Air Mobility Command (AMC). This command provides soldiers and supplies for airlift, air refueling, special air missions, and medical evacuation aircraft for U.S. forces during wartime.

AMC has around 150,000 members, and its aircraft are in the sky for tens of thousands of hours per month, bringing supplies or troops to the front lines. AMC also conducts air refueling, ensuring that other aircraft can accomplish their missions without having to land. AMC supervises the air force's aeromedical evacuation aircraft that bring wounded and dead U.S. service members back home. AMC is headquartered at Scott Air Force Base in Illinois and has one numbered unit, the 18th Air Force.

REGIONAL MAJCOMS

The oldest current air force MAJCOM, Pacific Air Forces (PACAF), operates out of Hickam Air Force Base in Hawaii. Established in 1944, PACAF organizes, trains, equips, and maintains resources to carry out air operations throughout the Asia-Pacific region during peacetime, crisis, and war. The PACAF's more than 50,000 airmen and women are stationed throughout Japan, South Korea, Alaska, and Guam.

U.S. Air Forces in Europe (USAFE) is the air force's other overseas MAJCOM. Headquartered at Ramstein Air Base in Germany, USAFE's AOR stretches all across Europe. There are more than 35,000 soldiers assigned to USAFE units all across the continent.

OTHER AIR FORCE UNITS

When not called to active federal duty, ANG airmen and women serve under the governors of the 50 states, Puerto Rico, Guam, the Virgin Islands, and the commanding general in the District of Columbia. Each governor is represented in their independent chain of command by an adjutant general. While ANG members train and prepare for war-related scenarios just like the rest of the air force, governors can call on the ANG to defend peace, order, and public safety. For example, guardsmen and women can provide assistance during emergencies, such as natural disasters. They are asked to conduct these missions because military troops at the federal level are not allowed to participate in law enforcement activities in the United States. During wartime or threats to national security, the president has the authority to call up ANG airmen and women to active duty.

More than 100,000 ANG members play a major part in the overall air force mission.

The air force structure also includes subdivisions called direct reporting units (DRUs). They report to air force headquarters at the Pentagon. DRUs are kept separate from MAJCOMs because they have unique missions and face different legal requirements. There are six DRUs with distinct responsibilities:

- The Air Force District of Washington at Joint Base Andrews, Maryland, brings air, space, and online capabilities to the joint team protecting the nation's capital.

- The Air Force Network Integration Center at Scott Air Force Base, Illinois, provides cyber simulation/validation and network standards, architecture, and engineering services.
- The Air Force Operational Test and Evaluation Center at various locations investigates and experiments with space and warfighting systems.
- The Air Reserve Personnel Center at Buckley Air Force Base, Colorado, is in charge of personnel support to nearly a million Air National Guard, Air Force Reserve, and retired members.
- The Arnold Air Force Base and Arnold Engineering Development Complex in Tullahoma, Tennessee, is the most advanced and largest complex of flight simulation test facilities in the world.
- The Air Force Academy in Colorado Springs, Colorado, is a military academy for officer candidates for the air force.

The air force also operates twelve field operating agencies (FOAs), which are air force subdivisions that complete activities under the control of a headquarters air force functional manager. One FOA is the Air Force Agency for Modeling and Simulation, based in Orlando, Florida. This agency develops new

In addition to standing by to help in times of conflict, air force reservists are always ready to lend a helping hand during an emergency.

tactics and planning. It also provides rehearsals and training programs before missions. Another FOA is the Air Force Public Affairs Agency in San Antonio, Texas, which provides airmen and women with special public affairs resources to document and convey the air force mission and legacy.

The U.S. Air Force is one of the nation's most important military units. It is no surprise that its structure is complex, with tens of thousands of soldiers and civilians spread all over the world. Within that organization, however, is a place for everyone, no matter the skill set they bring to the air force.

CHAPTER 5

AERIAL INCLUSION

As one of the youngest military divisions in the United States, the air force has a stronger history of diversity than some other branches. The air force has always been willing to break down barriers to make sure that it was able to recruit the best and brightest. Diversity and inclusion are major contributors to the undeniable strength of the military. Today, people of any race, gender, orientation, or background are welcome to join the air force in any number of specialty career paths.

WINGED WOMEN

While women have historically played support roles during military conflicts, they did not have an opportunity to participate in flight operations. The first hurdle women had to cross was proving that they were fit to fly. The United States has seen many inspirational women in the field of aviation. In 1886, Mary H. Myers set an altitude record by soaring 4 miles (6.4 km) above the earth in a balloon—without oxygen equipment. However, American women were not initially allowed to fly aircraft during World War I in England and the United States. In contrast, European women were used as pilots almost from the beginning of the war. In Germany, women were known to fly aircraft from factories to fields near the front lines. In Russia, women were even given

Though it took time for the United States to catch up, European women were showing their skills as pilots as early as World War I.

military ranks. The United States was somewhat behind the times, but by the 1920s and 1930s, American women such as Amelia Earhart had captivated the country with their airborne accomplishments.

Before long, Britain set an example by establishing a women's section of its Air Transport Auxiliary (ATA). Though women faced discrimination, made less money than male pilots, and had to pay for their own lodgings, ATA flight records revealed that the accident rates for men and women were nearly identical. During World War II, more than 100 women flew for the ATA.

In 1941, trailblazing pilot Jacqueline Cochran met Hap Arnold, a high-ranking army air force officer, in Washington, D.C. Arnold described the problem of ferrying bombers overseas, which was being done by civilians since military pilots were all used in combat. Cochran suggested using women in this role, and though Arnold originally did not believe a woman could handle it, he eventually agreed to allow Cochran to fly a bomber across the Atlantic in mid-1941.

Arnold encouraged Cochran to fly with the ATA, and she brought a small group of women to Britain to train. When Cochran returned to America in 1942, she was surprised to find that Nancy Harkness Love was forming the Women's Auxiliary Ferrying Squadron (WAFS). Cochran organized a Women's Flying Training Detachment from a field in Houston to train pilots for eventual service in the WAFS.

American pilot Jacqueline Cochran had made a name for herself in plane racing, but she wanted to help other female pilots get into the skies with the military.

WASPS IN THE AIR

On August 5, 1943, the ATA and the WAFS merged to become the Women Airforce Service Pilots (WASP). Cochran took the lead, and WASPs began to ferry aircraft to bases around the United States. WASPs were involved in many kinds of flying—but never combat.

The WASP program wound down when male military pilots began returning to the United States, resuming their ferrying responsibilities. Because of the success of the WASPs, however, Arnold was in favor of keeping the women pilots. Due to broader military restrictions that did not allow women to serve, Arnold was overruled. During its time, more than 1,000 WASP graduated training. These aviator women delivered 12,650 planes of 77 different types while suffering only 38 deaths.

After World War II, things began to change for women who wanted to serve in the military. In 1948, Congress passed the Women's Armed Forces Integration Act. Despite the fact that the total air forces could not be made up of more than 2 percent women and women could not be promoted above lieutenant colonel, women played a vital role during conflicts in the latter half of the 20th century. During the Korean War, female air force nurses served as flight nurses in Korea. Other servicewomen were assigned to duty in Japan.

In 1967, President Johnson approved Public Law 90-130, which opened up the military much more for women. The 2 percent cap on female soldiers was lifted, and women were allowed to join the ANG.

Soon after, the Air Force ROTC opened to women. In 1971, the air force promoted its first female brigadier general. In 1976, the Air Force Academy admitted the first female cadets. Soon, women began participating in pilot training and Test Pilot School.

By the 1980s, women were actively involved in global conflicts, such as in Grenada during Operation Urgent Fury. In 1986, six air force women served as pilots, copilots, and boom operators on the KC-135 and KC-10 tankers that refueled FB-111s during a raid on Libya. The same year, the Air Force Academy's top graduate was a woman.

In 1989, nearly 800 women participated in Operation Just Cause in Panama. Two earned the Air Medal with the "V" device, meaning that they served in combat. During Operations Desert Shield and Desert Storm, more than 40,000 air force women contributed to missions. In 1991, Congress repealed laws that prevented women from flying in active combat.

In 1993, Dr. Sheila Widnall was the first woman to be named secretary of the air force. As part of Operation Desert Fox in 1998, a female soldier was in the first wave of U.S. strikes against Iraq. By 2004, women in the air force were full participants in the war on terrorism, serving in many roles throughout the world. Though some positions are still not open to women, the Pentagon in 2015 announced that qualified soldiers—regardless of gender—would now be allowed to serve on the front lines in active combat roles.

Sheila Widnall made history as the first ever female service secretary in the United States.

FLYING FROM TUSKEGEE

Though Black soldiers have been serving in various branches of the U.S. armed forces since the nation's birth, they have often faced discrimination. For many years, young Black recruits were told that certain jobs were simply not open to them. Things began to change in 1941 with Executive Order 8802, which called for an end to discrimination within the military.

In 1941, the army air force established a program in Tuskegee, Alabama, to train Black Americans as military pilots at the Tuskegee Institute. The first classes of Tuskegee Airmen were trained to fly fighters.

More than a dozen men entered the class but only five successfully completed the training. One of them was Captain Benjamin O. Davis Jr., who would go on to become the air force's first Black general. Another

The Tuskegee Airmen made a major and immediate impact when they began flying in World War II.

famous Tuskegee Airman was Daniel "Chappie" James Jr., who would later become the air force's first Black general to reach a four-star rank.

The Tuskegee Airmen began overseas combat operations in World War II. They flew air patrols near Naples, Italy, and the Mediterranean Sea in early 1944. In April 1944, the group was moved closer to the Adriatic Sea and began conducting long-range heavy bomber escort missions for the 15th Strategic Air Force. In July 1944, the 99th Fighter Squadron was transferred to Ramitelli, and the group became the only four-squadron fighter group that was conducting bomber escort missions for the 15th Air Force.

Though a new program for training bomber pilots began in September 1943 at Tuskegee, World War II ended before these men saw combat. By the end of the war, nearly 1,000 men had graduated from pilot training at Tuskegee, about half of whom were sent overseas for combat assignment. During the same period, approximately 150 lost their lives while in training or on combat flights.

The Tuskegee Airmen served well, and they were highly celebrated because their squadron never lost a bomber to enemy attacks. They flew 15,000 combat sorties and destroyed more than 250 German airplanes.

Black Americans have served honorably in air force conflicts. Two Black soldiers were awarded the Medal of Honor during World War II, two during the Korean War, and twenty during the Vietnam War.

Today, Black Americans make up approximately 16 percent of the air force ranks. Some have attained ranks as high as four-star general. On May 15, 2005, Black airmen and women reached a significant milestone when Colonel Stayce Harris became the first Black woman to command a flying wing. She commanded the 459th Air Refueling Wing at Andrews Air Force Base in Maryland.

The air force has also produced accomplished Black astronauts, including Lieutenant Colonel Michael P. Anderson. Along with the crew of the space shuttle *Columbia*, Anderson died on February 1, 2003, when the vessel exploded. Anderson also flew aboard the space shuttle *Endeavour* in January 1998.

HISPANIC HISTORY IN THE AIR FORCE

People of color have always made significant contributions to national defense. Hispanic Americans have earned more Medals of Honor than any other ethnic minority, and Hispanic soldiers have been part of the defense of the United States since the American Revolution.

In 1929, Lieutenant General Elwood Quesada was among the first leaders to prove the importance of air refueling. He was a member of the famous "Question Mark" crew, which set a sustained in-flight refueling record of 151 hours while spending more than six days in the air over Los Angeles, California.

Air refueling operations take place when a tanker aircraft provides fuel to another aircraft in the sky using hoses, or "booms." The "Question Mark" plane flew 11,000 miles (17,700 km) without stopping and was air-refueled 43 times.

During World War II, around 500,000 Hispanic soldiers served in the U.S. armed forces. Oscar Perdomo, one such soldier, became the last ace of the war. Flying in a P-47N Thunderbolt near Okinawa on August 13, 1945, he encountered five Japanese aircraft and shot down three of them.

Later, he spotted two Japanese trainer aircraft and shot one down before encountering three more.

Hispanic American lieutenant general Elwood Quesada not only achieved a high rank, he was also a pioneer in air refueling missions.

In the combat that followed, Perdomo achieved his fifth confirmed kill of the day.

During the Korean War, Captain Manuel J. Fernandez, an F-86 fighter pilot, was credited with more than 14 enemy kills across 125 missions. He was the third-ranked fighter pilot of the war and retired as a colonel. In Vietnam, Air Force Master Sergeant Juan J. Valdez climbed aboard the last U.S. helicopter to depart the roof of the American Embassy in Saigon, marking the end of the U.S. presence in Vietnam. Hispanic soldiers also served valiantly during the Persian Gulf War. Today, they continue to serve in leadership positions in the air force and across the armed forces.

MORE EQUALITY FOR ALL

The modern military, backed by the federal government, formally recognizes many minority groups during special observances. These include Asian-Pacific heritage month in May, Disability Employment Awareness Month in October, and American Indian and Alaska Native Heritage Month in November.

Today, the U.S. military is improving its standards for gender and racial equality every day. Though there is always more work to be done, airmen and women from all over the world have proven that they can honorably serve in the air force. Because top leaders have recognized contributions from people of all backgrounds, the air force has become one of the world's most elite aerial fighting forces.

CHAPTER 6

LIVING IN THE AIR FORCE

One major advantage to a career in any armed service branch is the benefits package that the government provides to soldiers. The air force, especially, wants to take care of its airmen and women. In addition to a steady salary, the branch offers a comprehensive series of programs and incentives that is strong, even when compared to other military services. This compensation package is highly competitive with what is offered in the civilian world, making an air force occupation an appealing option to many.

WELCOME TO THE BASE

Most air force bases are like small U.S. towns. For starters, most have a shopping area with department stores and other smaller shops. Operated by the Army and Air Force Exchange Service (AAFES), the base exchange (or BX) offers tax-free shopping.

In addition, AAFES operates barbershops, fast food restaurants, and specialty shops. Bases commonly have restaurants, a grocery store (called the commissary), and gas stations.

Modern air force bases are much more than staging areas for aircraft takeoffs and landings.

For entertainment, bases offer onsite golf courses and movie theaters. Many have bowling alleys and nightclubs. Since the air force encourages good physical fitness, bases also have gyms. Air force bases also have basic facilities like schools, churches, and hospitals. Airmen and women living on or near the base have access to almost everything they would find in a civilian town.

Airmen and women are generally given the opportunity to live on base. If they do, the only services they have to pay for are services like cable, telephone, and internet access. Single enlisted members can stay in dorm-style rooms. Soldiers with families are offered two- to four-bedroom houses on most bases.

Those who live off base are given a tax-free allowance to help pay for rent or a mortgage. The amount of the allowance is based on rank, years of air force service, and location.

AIR FORCE ADVANTAGES

All air force soldiers are given 30 days of paid time off each year. When not in uniform, airmen and women can take advantage of travel opportunities offered on many military installations. For instance, they can take a transport-type aircraft to many places around the world for free if there is enough room on the scheduled flight.

Air force members wishing to continue their education can sign up for college courses offered on base by different institutions. The air force also offers a tuition-assistance program to help pay for school. The Montgomery G.I. Bill also provides tuition assistance and covers up to 36 months of benefits. These benefits may be used for degree and certificate programs, flight training, apprenticeship or on-the-job training, and other courses.

The air force offers an associate's degree—through the Community College of the Air Force (CCAF)—to enlisted members who want higher education. CCAF is the country's largest community college, and it is the only degree-granting institution in the world dedicated entirely to air force soldiers. Officers, who must already have at least a bachelor's degree, can get assistance to earn their master's or other advanced degree directly related to their specialty from the Air Force Institute of Technology.

FOR COUNTRY AND COMMUNITY

Since bases are generally located near major towns and cities, the air force actively seeks ways to be involved in the community. Each base has a public affairs office that is responsible for earning the public's trust and maintaining support for the base and the air force. One easy way to get civilians interested is to offer air force base tours for community groups. In addition, most bases host airshows that can attract thousands of people to see aerial demonstrations and antique aircraft.

In addition to public affairs programs through the air force, airmen and women are typically independently involved in activities like school organizations, coaching, and volunteering with community centers and nonprofit organizations, as well as tutoring.

The air force participates in many community-engagement programs to give civilians a chance to interact with the soldiers who protect them.

ENLISTING IN THE AIR FORCE

Before anyone can receive the benefits and privileges of being a U.S. airman or woman, they must take an important step. Deciding whether to enlist in the air force can be one of the biggest decisions in a young person's life.

Once the decision has been made, joining the air force is a fairly simple process. Applicants must be at least 17 but younger than 40. Air force recruiters can be found in most cities, and online, to assist potential recruits and answer questions.

The air force requires recruits to have a high school diploma or a general equivalency diploma (GED). Early on, recruits must take the Armed Services Vocational Aptitude Battery (ASVAB). The ASVAB is broken down into four categories: mechanical, administrative, general, and electronic. An overall score of 36 is the minimum for a high school graduate; a score of 65 is required for someone with a GED. Each special air force career field also sets minimum score requirements.

Once accepted, air force recruits are sent to a Military Entrance Processing Station, where they undergo a full physical examination. Recruits are fingerprinted and interviewed by a counselor to help match their ASVAB scores with the needs of the air force.

They are then sent to basic military training (BMT) at Lackland Air Force Base in Texas. This six-week course includes physical fitness training, classroom instruction, field training, and education on air force customs.

The first week is designed to provide many mental and physical challenges. Days begin at 5:00 a.m., and there are few breaks in between conditioning exercises, book learning, and practical studies. Physical fitness is a major part of getting through BMT. Trainees must pass two physical conditioning tests that consist of running, push-ups, and sit-ups in order to graduate.

Like in all U.S. armed service branches, air force recruits must graduate a tough basic training program before they begin their military careers.

Over the following few weeks, trainees are taught about the structure, ethics, and values of the air force. They participate in field training and run obstacle courses that build confidence. They are also given firearms training, learning how to shoot and clean the standard-issue rifle. Trainees can earn their first uniform ribbon by qualifying as an "expert" shooter during this training.

In 1999, the air force introduced Warrior Week as a final test to simulate the reality of deployments recruits are likely to face. Historically, the air force has not made a major effort to teach enlisted members general soldiering skills. Since the Cold War ended, the air force has become smaller—but more airmen are being deployed to dangerous places.

During Warrior Week, trainees learn how to erect tents, put on protective equipment for chemical warfare, and provide basic first aid. The whole week is constructed around an actual mission to defend the base from invasion by the enemy (a role played by the instructors).

After graduation, airmen and women are sent to receive technical training for the job, or specialty, to which they were assigned. These programs are primarily conducted at Keesler Air Force Base in Mississippi or in Texas at Goodfellow Air Force Base, Lackland Air Force Base, or Sheppard Air Force Base. For example, those in computer-related fields normally go to Keesler Air Force Base for training. Some specialized training occurs on the bases of other armed services, such as the Defense

Information School at Fort Meade in Maryland for those entering the public affairs career field. Depending on the specialty, training can take anywhere from a few weeks to a full year. After they have completed their technical training, airmen and women are sent to their first duty station.

GETTING COMPENSATED

One of the positives of working for the U.S. armed forces is that there are no questions about yearly salaries. Enlisted airmen and women earn money based on rank and years of service. Paychecks come twice per month. Enlisted ranks go from airman basic (grade E-1) through chief master sergeant (grade E-9).

This basic pay is only one part of a soldier's total compensation. The air force pays special bonuses for those who serve in career fields that are highly stressful or experiencing shortages of people. Enlisted airmen and women without families are also provided free room and board and a clothing allowance. It is also possible to earn extra pay for hazardous duties or speaking another language. Married soldiers living off base are provided extra money for food and housing, and these allowances are not taxed. The air force also offers a generous retirement plan, allowing soldiers to retire with up to 50 percent of their final base salary after 20 years of active-duty service. The air force also provides optional life insurance benefits for a small monthly price.

After accounting for free medical and dental benefits, year-round gym access, tax-free shopping, educational benefits, and recreation programs, the total air force compensation package is competitive with other career choices.

Airmen and women also have many opportunities for promotion to higher ranks. Each year, soldiers are evaluated by their supervisors in an Enlisted Performance Review. Promotions are partly based on awards and decorations. Medals include the Defense Service Medal and the Medal of Honor, and the more common Good Conduct Medal, Achievement Medal, and Meritorious Service Medal. Many who serve with honor while in direct contact with the enemy have earned the Bronze Star. Those hurt or killed in action are awarded the Purple Heart.

Soldiers who go above and beyond during their air force service can be awarded special medals, including the Bronze Star, which is given to soldiers who perform heroic actions.

TAKING OFFICE

Enlisted airmen and women form the backbone of the air force, but the branch's officers are where it sets itself apart. Every commissioned officer in the air force must have at least a four-year college degree. Officers take unit command and operational career paths, such as pilots, navigators, and battle management jobs. Officers must complete the Air Force Officer Qualifying Test (AFOQT), a written exam similar to the SAT. The AFOQT is used to select applicants for officer commissioning programs, such as the U.S. Air Force Academy (USAFA), OTS, or ROTC. It also sets requirement for selection into specific training programs, including pilot and navigator training.

The AFOQT can only be taken twice, and candidates must wait 180 days between tests. Certain career fields have minimum scores. For example, aspiring pilots must score at least a 25 on the pilot section, which measures knowledge of aviation and mechanical systems, the ability to read aircraft instruments, and other flight-related knowledge.

Some highly qualified young people receive training at the USAFA, located in Colorado Springs, Colorado. The USAFA is one of the nation's top undergraduate institutions for those who want to join the military. Cadets complete four years of studies, graduating with a bachelor of science degree. The school focuses on academics, military training, athletic conditioning, and spiritual and ethical development.

Academics include courses in engineering, social sciences, and military studies. Cadets can select from more than 30 majors. The USAFA also fields men's and women's sports teams that compete with other colleges around the nation. The school's physical education program comprises mandatory courses in general physical fitness and electives ranging from judo to SCUBA.

Upon graduation from the USAFA, cadets receive commissions as second lieutenants. Most must make a five-year commitment to the active-duty air force. Pilots must make a 10-year commitment.

The USAFA is selective, and the process of getting accepted starts in high school. Young students should work to achieve good grades, participate in extracurricular activities, and demonstrate good leadership. About 85 percent of USAFA cadets finished in the top quarter of their high school class—and more than 10 percent graduated at the top of their high school class. Getting good scores on standardized tests, including the SAT and ACT, is important.

Candidates must also meet with an Air Force Academy admissions liaison officer (ALO) or another representative of the school. These meetings give young people an opportunity to make a good first impression and ask any questions they may have about the USAFA or military service in general.

THE ROTC AND OCS OPTIONS

The Air Force ROTC is open to full-time students at more than 1,100 colleges and universities in the United States and Puerto Rico. Because it is offered nationwide, ROTC is the largest supplier of officers to the armed forces. Credit for a portion of the first year of the four-year program may be provided for completion of at least two years of junior ROTC—a high school version of the program—participation in the Civil Air Patrol, military school training, or prior U.S. military service.

Thousands of ROTC scholarships are available to help pay for either full or partial tuition, books, and laboratory fees. Though these scholarships are available for any degree program, those with scientific and technical-related majors are often given priority.

An aspiring air force member already in college can also join ROTC, provided they have at least a 2.5 GPA and are a U.S. citizen. They must also receive good scores on the AFOQT, pass a physical fitness test, and meet the ROTC weight and body fat standards. They must also pass a physical examination and review board.

Once accepted, underclassmen cadets (freshmen and sophomores) enter the General Military Course, which teaches them about the development of airpower and the air force's structure. Students take courses in aerospace studies. AS100 is the student's first introduction to the air force. The AS200 course

Young men and women who join Air Force ROTC programs have a chance to prepare for a potential career in the armed services.

focuses on the history of airpower and how politics can affect the use of military power.

Upperclassmen enter the Professional Officer Course, which covers air force leadership and management, as well as U.S. defense policy. AS300 teaches the skills needed to be a successful leader and manager. Case studies on leadership are discussed, and cadets are given problem-solving exercises. AS400 examines national security policies, methods of managing conflict, alliances and regional security agreements, and analysis of the threats of war.

In addition to academic classes, all cadets participate in Leadership Laboratory, or "Lead Lab." This program provides cadets with an opportunity to develop leadership skills and use their classroom knowledge. Cadets are exposed to air force customs, courtesies, drills, and ceremonies, including marching and how to properly wear their uniforms. Lead Lab also offers field trips to air force bases and air force officer guest speakers, who help educate cadets about air force careers and experiences.

During the summer between their sophomore and junior years, cadets are sent to field training, the ROTC version of BMT. Field training is a four- or six-week course that gives cadets a taste of military life and teaches them the skills of a leader. This intensive course pushes cadets to their physical and mental limits. After successfully completing field training, cadets return to their campus and sign an agreement to continue in the program. Cadets are allowed to take ROTC for two years and go through field training before they have to sign an official contract and make a commitment to the air force.

After graduation, cadets are commissioned as second lieutenants in the air force and start down one of the career paths they have indicated they would like to follow. Those who qualify to be pilots must serve for 10 years after they complete a yearlong flight training course. Navigators must serve five years after navigator training, plus a two-year inactive reserve commitment. Nonflying officers serve four years of active duty with a four-year inactive reserve commitment.

Another way to earn a commission in the U.S. Air Force is through the OTS at Maxwell Air Force Base in Alabama. OTS provides a nine-and-a-half-week course of basic officer training that is designed to train and commission 1,000 officers each year. Additionally, OTS conducts a four-week commissioned officer training program to teach leadership skills to more than 1,500 newly commissioned judge advocates, chaplains, and medical officers each year. OTS is a good option for those with the talent and drive to become a leader in the air force.

THE REWARDS OF LEADERSHIP

Because of their increased responsibility and accountability, officers generally receive better compensation than enlisted members. Officer ranks go from second lieutenant to general, and each rank has an associated pay grade. For example, a second lieutenant has an O-1 grade while a general has an O-10 grade. There are four different levels of generals. A brigadier general has one star, a major general two, a lieutenant general three, and a general has four stars on their uniform.

Officers taking on careers as pilots, navigators, and doctors receive extra pay for their special duties to help ensure that their pay is similar to what they could receive outside of the military. Otherwise, it would be difficult to recruit officers in these careers, which can pay high salaries for civilians.

Similar to enlisted members, officers have a retirement plan, are given extra pay for hazardous duties, receive life insurance and medical and dental coverage, and are provided other benefits, such as travel incentives and 30 days of vacation time.

NOT AN EASY JOB

The benefits and pay for air force members are appealing, but the military is not without its challenges and risks. Basic training is enough to stop some recruits in their tracks. After training, the air force often moves its forces and people all around the world. As a result, most airmen and women will find themselves directly involved in an overseas conflict at one point or another. In the past, pilots were most at risk of being killed by the enemy in combat. Today, the air force focuses more on operations. This means people who are not pilots are also being sent to the frontlines. Anyone who joins the air force could potentially be deployed to an area where soldiers are in danger of being injured or killed.

Many people who join the military do so because they want to defend their country. For others, the most important thing is achieving a steady and healthy lifestyle for their family. The air force offers recruits the opportunity to learn, serve, and build a better life. Though the rewards can be excellent, there are also many risks. Anyone considering a career in the air force should spend a lot of time thinking over their options to make sure they are comfortable with their choice.

CHAPTER 7

AIR FORCE OCCUPATIONS

Most people think of pilots when the air force comes to mind, but pilots make up only a small percentage of total airmen and women. There are many different occupations and specialties available to members of the air force, ranging from direct aircraft involvement to technical operations at a base. There are countless support roles that help keep the air force flying on a daily basis.

ENLISTED CAREERS

Enlisted airmen and women typically have four main career paths to choose from: mechanical, administrative, general, and electronics. Each one serves a necessary purpose for the military.

The air force develops and operates extremely sophisticated and complicated equipment, and there is always a need for people with the mechanical skills to maintain them. Soldiers in a mechanical career field could be working as aircraft mechanics or dealing with radio systems, weapons, or vehicles.

Aircraft mechanics do everything from repairing engines to inspecting and operating ejection seats. Aircraft mechanics are just as important as pilots are, and without them, it would be difficult for air force planes to even get off the ground. Mechanics work in set crews and typically specialize in a particular type of airplane.

The mechanical career area also has some unique opportunities, such as working as an aerial gunner on an airplane or helicopter. Aerial gunners participate in missions like operating a weapon system on a helicopter while searching for a downed pilot. Gunners are placed on flying status as aircrew members, which means that they earn flight and hazardous duty pay.

Another unique job is a missile and space systems maintenance apprentice. Airmen and women in these positions maintain, assemble, and inspect the nation's intercontinental ballistic missiles (ICBMs).

Modern planes are incredible pieces of engineering, and that means they require dedicated professionals to maintain their combat worthiness.

ICBMs are always on alert to retaliate against enemies thousands of miles away. These powerful weapons are only effective if they are well maintained.

Enlisted soldiers with administrative careers are responsible for many day-to-day base operations. They help provide the food, equipment, and housing that are critical to air force operations.

One exciting career in administration is airfield management. Airmen and women in this role have a major effect on a pilot's ability to land, take off, and taxi on runways throughout the world. Airfield managers inspect airfields worldwide, supervise construction projects, and issue important flight notices to airmen and women regarding hazards or restrictions that could pose flight-safety problems. If the airfield managers say something is not safe, all flying stops.

The air force offers more than 70 types of general occupations that are less mechanical or technical in nature. These include working in air traffic control, communicating in other languages as a linguist, or collecting and analyzing intelligence.

One of the many advantages of today's air force is its highly advanced weapons systems and aircraft. The electronics that run this technology are always becoming smaller and more powerful—and they always require well-trained soldiers to operate and maintain them. Airmen and women in an electronics career field are trained to work with radar, avionics systems, surveillance systems, and missile and space systems.

INFLIGHT MEDICINE

Jobs in the medical field can also be classified as general. In these careers, airmen and women could work at a laboratory, in a clinic or pharmacy, or as medical-support personnel inside an emergency room or in a war zone helping to treat wounded soldiers. For example, an aeromedical apprentice assists in the care of patients during emergency medical flights as an airborne emergency medical technician. An aeromedical apprentice would work closely with a flight surgeon to ensure that pilots and navigators, missile alert crewmembers, and air traffic control staff are healthy and prepared for duty. They may also assist in some surgical procedures.

For example, following a training course at Lackland or Sheppard Air Force Bases in Texas, a bomber avionics systems instrument and flight control apprentice would perform operational checks and fix malfunctions of flight control systems on either the B-2 stealth bomber or the B-1. They would be responsible for several of the bomber's advanced aircraft systems, including the automatic pilot, flight controls, navigation, and hydraulic system indicators.

Understanding weather has always been a major part of successful military operations. Without accurate weather predictions, missions could fail because planes might not take off or land safely, or targets might not be visible to a gunner using nonradar weapons. In the air force, a weather apprentice

Just as radar did during World War II, computers have changed the face of modern warfare. The air force employs many soldiers who operate these electronics.

would be expected to analyze and forecast weather and space conditions for military decision makers. Weather apprentices receive scientific training to understand Earth's atmosphere and how to predict changes using satellite, radar, and computers.

OFFICER OPTIONS

Just like enlisted airmen and women, air force officers have a wide variety of specialties from which to choose. Their paths typically fall into one of four categories: flight, nontechnical, specialty, and technical.

Without the power of flight, there would be no air force. Air crews, however, are made up of more than just pilots. There are career opportunities for navigators, air battle managers, radar navigators, and weapons navigators.

Pilots or navigators are found flying in any class of aircraft: fighter, reconnaissance, surveillance, bomber, or airlift. Those selected as pilot candidates attend a yearlong Joint Specialized Undergraduate Pilot Training (JSUPT) course. Civilian flight instructors conduct this training in aircraft such as the Cessna 152. Students receive 50 hours of instruction and must qualify for a private pilot certificate.

The JSUPT program is conducted with the navy at Vance Air Force Base in Oklahoma and Naval Air Station Whiting Field in Florida. Students complete primary flight training in the air force's T-37B and the navy's T-34. Other students complete the primary

Earning one's wings is one of the most important moments of a military career. U.S. Air Force pilots are among the best and brightest officers in the world.

training at Columbus Air Force Base in Mississippi, or Laughlin Air Force Base in Texas, flying the T-37B.

After the first section of JSUPT, students move to more advanced training. Trainees selected for fighter-bomber planes train in the T-38A. Those selected as airlift-tanker pilots complete their training in the T-1A at Columbus AFB in Mississippi, Laughlin Air Force Base in Texas, or Vance Air

Force Base in Oklahoma. In these programs, they learn about air-to-air refueling, airdrop missions, and navigation.

Students selected to fly the massive C-130 Hercules transport craft train with the T-44 turboprop trainer at Naval Air Station Corpus Christi in Texas. Other students are selected to fly helicopters, and their training takes place at Fort Rucker in Alabama, where they use the UH-1 Huey to learn skills such as low-level flying,

Though pilots are the most well-known air force members, other nontechnical positions require talented people who can demonstrate leadership. Opportunities are available in areas such as air force intelligence, personnel, security forces, and communications. There are also opportunities as a space operations officer, controlling one of the air force's multibillion-dollar space systems or helping launch a variety of satellites into orbit.

One unit, the 7th Space Warning Squadron at Beale Air Force Base in California, works inside a 10-story, pyramid-like structure that makes up one huge radar system called Precision Acquisition of Vehicle Entry Phased Array Warning System (PAVE PAWS). This system continuously scans the horizon to detect and track sea-launched ballistic missiles and ICBMs headed toward North America.

Since it was developed in the 1980s, there have been no enemy missiles for PAVE PAWS to track, so the men and women who work in this unit have another mission: they provide space surveillance and

The Beale Air Force Base features this Upgraded Early Warning Radar, which can detect threats from missiles on Earth and objects in space.

track objects in Earth's orbit. The data they collect is used to create a satellite catalog database that includes nearly 30,000 man-made objects in orbit. Nearly 10,000 of these require careful monitoring to prevent them from colliding with other satellites or space shuttles.

Officers in the air force also have access to highly specialized careers that require specific skills. Among these specialty jobs are judge advocate, special investigative officer, and band officer.

The specialty occupational area also comprises base chaplains, who provide religious support to air force personnel. Chaplains develop and administer chaplain service policies, provide professional religious support, and advise commanders on religious, ethical, moral, morale, and quality-of-life issues.

Though only a few specialties fall under this category, technical careers are critical to the success of the air force. Technical careers include acquisition manager, aerospace engineer, mechanical engineer, scientist, and weather officer.

One specialty that has become increasingly important in the air force is the civil engineer. The air force often finds itself in areas overseas that have no existing infrastructure. The military refers to these as "bare base" locations. Civil engineers design and maintain the buildings and utilities to operate in a new location. They specialize in areas including architectural, electrical, mechanical, and environmental engineering. Civil engineers turn a bare base into a fully functional military installation, complete with sleeping quarters, command-and-control buildings, functioning runways, and working water, power, and other utilities.

Air force civil engineers are good at building new offices, homes, and other structures, but other engineers specialize in developing new ways at tearing down these buildings behind enemy lines. The Air Force Combat Ammunition Center, operating out of Beale Air Force Base in California, offers a program specifically designed to help engineers understand how to manage ammunition transportation and production when operating abroad.

CHAPTER 8

THE FUTURE OF AIR WARFARE

The modern U.S. Air Force stands alone as the most powerful aerial fighting force in the world. Because the air force is so powerful, it is unlikely that future wars will reach the same scale as 20th-century conflicts like World War II. It does not mean, however, that conflicts do not break out. The new face of warfare is local or regional, and the air force is always ready to respond to these threats.

MODERN WARFARE

Enemies around the globe still fight the United States and its allies using terrorism, often attacking with unconventional weapons. In the modern age, enemy weapons can take the form of unmanned aerial vehicles (UAVs, or drones), cyber warfare, or chemical weapons. To keep up with this diversity of threats, the air force must be a responsive force. It remains committed to the AEF concept, and about 30,000 airmen and women are deployed globally at a time.

In cooperation with the relatively young U.S. Space Force, the U.S. Air Force continues to include space operations in military planning. The United States has taken the lead in making space a new battlefield. Space-based systems were a major part of Operations Enduring Freedom and Iraqi Freedom. For example, soldiers used satellite feeds to identify and strike the broadcast capabilities of Iraqi state-run television. This information from space was sent to Predator UAVs, which then fired Hellfire missiles, successfully destroying the key source of Saddam Hussein's propaganda.

COMMUNICATION AND TECHNOLOGY

Intelligence has always been a major part of warfare. As data and computers continue to take over the world, protecting information and communication systems is an area of increasing importance for the air force. Because the air force relies on computers and global networks for nearly all of its functions, these systems are potentially vulnerable.

In addition to investing in defensive measures, the air force continues to develop newer weapons, including aircraft, delivery systems, and other technologies to give airmen and women the edge in combat. Some, like improvements to UAVs, help soldiers avoid flying into highly defended enemy airspace altogether.

One class of UAV, the RQ-4 Global Hawk, debuted during the war in Afghanistan in 2002. It flies at altitudes above 60,000 feet (18.3 km). Though it does not capture live video like the Predator, the RQ-4 can capture images at night or through bad weather. It can fly for nearly a day and a half

ATTACKS FROM ABOVE

One UAV, the Predator, is used to conduct a variety of missions over hostile territory. It is equipped with cameras that can transmit live footage of enemy actions to a commander on the ground or a fighter aircraft overhead. Information from Predator UAVs allows commanders to take out targets faster than ever before.

In the late 1990s, the air force began investigating UAVs armed with Hellfire missiles in combat in Iraq. The results were mixed. The Predator did its job, but the Hellfire missile was not a powerful enough weapon to take out large targets. One result of this testing was that the air force continued to develop other armed UAVs.

The Predator is one of the most well-known UAVs because of its widespread use in Middle Eastern conflicts.

without refueling and can send real-time images to battlefield commanders.

In addition to advances in UAV technology, the air force still develops manned aircraft. After years of extensive testing, the F-22—meant to replace the F-15 as the nation's top air-to-air fighter—was declared ready for war in 2005. F-22s can now be seen streaking across the sky in combat. F-22s were initially based at Langley Air Force Base in Virginia, home to the famed 1st Fighter Wing.

Though the air force is often at the cutting edge of technological advancements, everything developed by the service is meant to be shared with the other armed forces branches. Training exercises, such as the Combined Joint Training Force Exercise, run out of Langley Air Force Base, combine elements of the U.S. military with forces from the United Kingdom, Canada, the Netherlands, Norway, France, Germany, and Peru to train using realistic scenarios.

PEOPLE POWER

Even with all the high-tech options in the world, the air force recognizes that no weapon, system, or aircraft can be successfully operated without people. As a result, taking care of its members continues to be the air force's top priority. Airmen and women carry out missions and ensure the success and future of the U.S. Air Force.

Though the air force does not anticipate full-scale aerial engagements in the foreseeable future, it still requires a steady stream of new recruits to keep itself fully functional. The branch's top leaders are always looking at ways to improve the consistency of enlistment numbers so that bases can stay operational for years to come. As new technology continues to develop, the need for qualified, passionate people will only increase. For any young person who has an interest in the military, the air force is a solid, steady option. From piloting an F-22 to administrating a global air force base, there are occupational paths available for anyone who is willing to work hard and serve their nation.

GLOSSARY

ace Military pilot who shoots down five or more enemy aircraft.

air refueling Aircraft receiving fuel from another aircraft in mid-flight.

base exchange (BX) Shopping facility on most bases that resembles a department store.

blockade The blocking by military forces of access to a place in order to prevent the entry of goods.

close air support Air action against hostile targets close to friendly ground or naval forces requiring detailed integration of fire and movement.

coalition A temporary alliance of distinct parties, persons, or states for joint action.

collateral damage Unintentional damage to things or people in the vicinity of an intended target.

combat air patrol Aerial fighting position over a target or location.

deploy To be sent overseas to support a military operation.

ethnic Of a racial group or member of such a group.

munition A weapon, like a bomb or missile.

precision-guided munition A weapon guided to its target by satellite or radar.

psychological operations Using information against the enemy to destroy its morale or will to fight.

reconnaissance Collecting information or intelligence on an enemy.

sortie One flight by an aircraft.

squadron Basic military unit made up of multiple flights.

stealth An airplane's ability to evade detection by radar.

strategy The planning and directing of the whole operation of a campaign or war.

ultimatum A final warning or order.

Air Force Reserve
Robins Air Force Base
Highway 247
Robins AFB, Georgia 31098
Website: afreserve.com
Facebook and Instagram:
@AirForceReserveRecruiting
Twitter: @Join_AFReserve
The official website of the Air Force Reserve contains information about choosing a career as a reservist, including the qualifications, requirements, and commitments necessary for a new recruit.

Military.com: Air Force
133 Boston Post Road
Weston, MA 02493
Website: www.military.com/air-force
Facebook, Instagram, and Twitter:
@Militarydotcom
Military.com provides information on all things U.S. military, and its air force page has details on current events, breaking news, and general statistics and data related to working in the air force.

National Museum of the United States Air Force

1100 Spaatz Street
Wright-Patterson AFB, Ohio 45433
Website: www.nationalmuseum.af.mil
Facebook and Twitter: @AFmuseum
The official museum of the air force combines the branch's rich history with its bright future, providing information about famous moments in aviation and cutting-edge developments.

United States Air Force

1400 Defense Pentagon
Washington, DC 20301-1400
Website: www.airforce.com
Facebook: @USAirForceRecruiting
Instagram and Twitter: @USAFRecruiting
The official website of the U.S. Air Force has information for young people who are thinking about joining, including instructions on how to apply and what the requirements are.

United States Air Force Academy

2304 Cadet Drive, Suite 3100
USAF Academy, CO 80840-5002
Website: www.usafa.edu
Facebook: @USAFA.Official
Instagram and Twitter: @AF_Academy
The premier educational institution for those who want to become air force officers, the USAFA maintains a website with news about the school and information on how to apply.

FOR FURTHER READING

Abdo, Kenny. *United States Air Force*. Minneapolis, MN: Abdo Zoom, 2019.

Boothroyd, Jennifer. *Inside the U.S. Air Force*. Minneapolis, MN: Lerner Publications, 2018.

Conkling, Winifred, and Julia Kuo. *Heroism Begins with Her: Inspiring Stories of Bold, Brave, and Gutsy Women in the U.S. Military*. New York, NY: Harper, 2019.

Dakers, Diane. *Amelia Earhart: Pioneering Aviator and Force for Women's Rights*. New York, NY: Crabtree Publishing, 2016.

Hegar, Mary Jennings. *Fly Like a Girl: One Woman's Dramatic Flight in Afghanistan and on the Home Front*. New York, NY: Penguin, 2020.

Hustad, Douglas. *Life in the U.S. Air Force*. San Diego, CA: ReferencePoint Press, 2021.

Macon, Franklin J., and Elizabeth G. Harper. *I Wanted to Be a Pilot: The Making of a Tuskegee Airman*. New York, NY: Morgan James Publishing, 2019.

Marsh, Richard Lee, and Jason Bach. *ABCs of the Air Force*. Herndon, VA: Mascot Books, 2017.

Mitchell, P. P. *Join the Air Force*. New York, NY: Gareth Stevens, 2018.

Murray, Julie. *Air Force Pararescue*. Minneapolis, MN: Dash! 2021.

O'Brien, Cynthia. *Air Force Careers*. New York, NY: Crabtree, 2021.

Phillips, Howard. *Inside Pararescue*. New York, NY: PowerKids Press, 2022.

Phillips, Melissa A. *Careers in the US Air Force*. San Diego, CA: ReferencePoint Press, 2016.

Ringstad, Arnold. *US Air Force: Equipment and Vehicles*. Minneapolis, MN: Kids Core, 2022.

Russo, Kristin J. *Surprising Facts About Being an Air Force Airman*. North Mankato, MN: Capstone Press, 2018.

Settle, Jimmy, and Don Rearden. *Never Quit: How I Became a Special Ops Pararescue Jumper*. New York, NY: St. Martin's Griffin, 2018.

INDEX

A

aerospace expeditionary forces (AEFs), 29–31
air force bases, life on, 59–60
Air Force Reserve (AFR), 30–31, 32, 36, 39, 44
Air Force ROTC, 36, 51, 68, 70–73
Air National Guard (ANG), 31, 32, 36, 42, 50
Anderson, Michael P., 55
Arnold, Henry H. "Hap," 16, 48, 50

B

Bleckley, Erwin, 7
Bush, George H. W., 24, 28

C

Clinton, Bill, 25, 28
Cochran, Jacqueline, 48, 49, 50
Cold War, 16, 18, 65
Coolidge, Calvin, 11
Cuban Missile Crisis, 20

D

Davis, Benjamin O., 53
direct reporting units (DRUs), 42–43
Doolittle, Jimmy, 13–14

F

Fernandez, Manuel J., 57
field operating agencies (FOAs), 43–45

G

Goettler, Harold, 7

ABOUT THE AUTHOR

Kyle Purrman is a former heart surgeon who has a passion for storytelling through education. This is his first book for young adults; most of his previous publications are in scientific literature.

CREDITS

Designer: Michael Flynn; Editor: Siyavush Saidian